P9-DGS-731

# SCIENCE DETECTIVES

## Investigating
# Why Leaves Change Their Color

Ellen René

PowerKiDS
press.

New York

*To my daughter, Emily, who colors my life with love and laughter*

Published in 2009 by The Rosen Publishing Group, Inc.
29 East 21st Street, New York, NY 10010

First Edition

Editor: Joanne Randolph
Book Design: Julio Gil
Photo Researcher: Jessica Gerweck

Photo Credits: Cover, back cover (top center, top right, middle left, bottom left), pp. 5, 6, 9, 10, 13, 14, 17, 18, 21 Shutterstock.com; back cover (middle center) © Jim Merli; back cover (middle right) © Fat Chance Productions.

Library of Congress Cataloging-in-Publication Data

René, Ellen.
  Investigating why leaves change their color / Ellen Rene. — 1st ed.
       p. cm. — (Science detectives)
  Includes index.
  ISBN 978-1-4042-4485-6 (library binding)
  1. Leaves—Color—Juvenile literature. 2.  Fall foliage—Juvenile literature. I. Title.
  QK649.R46 2009
  575.5'7—dc22

                                                    2008003885

Manufactured in the United States of America

# Contents

# Out of Thin Air

Have you ever looked up at a tall, leafy tree and wondered, "How did it get so big?" For a long time scientists did not know. They thought plants, like animals, had to "eat" to grow. The scientists guessed that plants "ate" something in soil.

Today we know that plants build themselves mostly from the air. That is where they get **carbon**, a building block for life. The carbon plants use comes from **carbon dioxide**, a gas in the air. Plants turn carbon dioxide and water into food. This is called **photosynthesis**, and it takes place inside green leaves. Why green leaves, you might ask? What about when leaves change their color?

You likely see big, green, leafy trees, like this one, all the time. Did you ever stop to wonder why leaves look green, though?

Sunlight

Oxygen

Carbon Dioxide

Water

This picture shows how photosynthesis works. The plant takes in water, carbon dioxide, and sunlight, and it gives off oxygen.

# What Is Photosynthesis?

Plants need energy, or power, to live and grow. They get it from sugar, the energy-rich food they make. Where does the energy stored in sugar come from? That energy comes from the Sun. "Photosynthesis" means "putting together by light." Sunlight helps plants put carbon dioxide and water together to make sugars and other **carbohydrates**. The plant gives off **oxygen**, the gas we breathe.

Plants have to trap sunlight before they can use it, though. How do they do that? They have a powerful, green "superhero" in their leaves. It saves the day, or really, daylight. This plant superhero is **chlorophyll**!

# Chlorophyll and Sunlight

Mixing light is not the same as mixing paint. The three primary light colors are red, green, and blue. Red and blue light mix to make magenta. Red and green make yellow. Blue and green make a color called cyan. Mixing all primary light colors together makes white light.

Chlorophyll traps sunlight and helps plants use the energy it holds. People use sunlight's energy, too. We need it to keep us warm and we need it to see. The Sun makes its own light. Most things do not. Sunlight looks white to us. It is really made up of waves of many different colors, though.

An object's color depends on the light waves it **reflects**, or sends, back to our eyes. White objects reflect all colors of light. Black objects take in, or absorb, all colors of light. Chlorophyll absorbs most sunlight. It reflects green waves, though, so it looks green.

These lemons look yellow to our eyes because they take in all the colors except yellow. The yellow color gets reflected back to us.

Here you can see some leaves that are colored green, yellow, and red. Pigments in the leaves cause each of these colors.

# What Makes Leaf Colors?

**Pigments** color living things. They absorb and reflect different waves of light so an apple looks red and a sunflower looks yellow. Three groups of pigments color leaves.

Chlorophyll colors leaves green. **Carotenoids** color them mostly yellow and orange. Both groups are found in leaves all through the growing season. **Anthocyanins** are made in fall. They color leaves red and purple.

Pigments do more than color leaves. They help leaves carry on life processes. The carotenoids help out with photosynthesis. They catch light and pass it to chlorophyll.

Tannins are waste from plant cells. They build up in dying leaves and color them brown. Scientists also think tannins are made to keep plants safe from bugs and animals that eat leaves.

# Sun Catchers

Some plants track the Sun. They turn their leaves to catch its most direct rays. As the Sun moves across the sky during the day, the plants' leaves move to follow the Sun.

Leaves come in different shapes and sizes. Some leaves grow as long as railroad cars. Others fit on the head of a pin. All carry on photosynthesis. The way they are built helps them do this job.

Most leaves have two parts, a blade and a stalk. The thin stalk fixes it to the plant. The wider blade helps leaves catch sunlight and take in carbon dioxide. Gases move in and out of leaves through tiny openings, or pores. A thin, waxy coating covers most leaves. It keeps them safe and keeps them from drying out.

# Deciduous Leaf

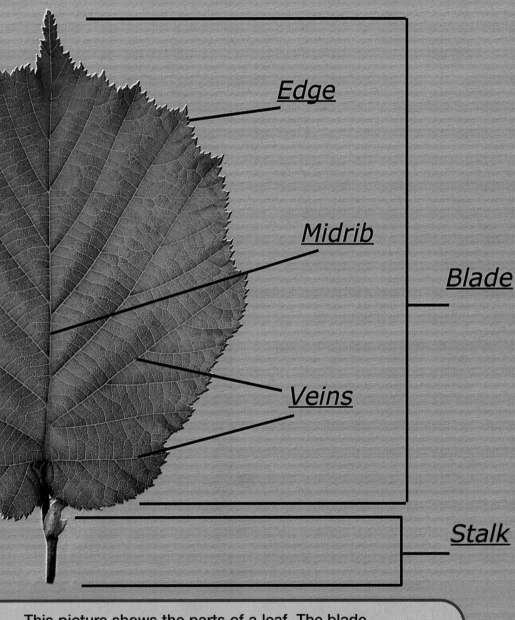

Edge

Midrib

Blade

Veins

Stalk

This picture shows the parts of a leaf. The blade
has lines running through it called veins.

Here you can see all the veins running through the leaf.
Veins help move food and water through the plant.

# How Do Plants Move Food Around?

Roots take in water and **minerals** from soil. Leaves make food and other matter. How do things move around inside plants? They move through a system of tubes. One kind of tube moves water and minerals up from roots to leaves.

Another kind of tube moves food from the leaves to where it is needed. Leaves use some of the sugars they make in photosynthesis. Extra food goes to other plant parts, like stems and roots, where it is used or stored. The two kinds of tubes are the veins you see on leaves.

# Hidden Color

During the growing season, photosynthesis goes on full blast. Leaves make lots of chlorophyll. They need a steady supply. Sunlight breaks chlorophyll down. This happens in the same way that sunlight fades colored paper or cloth over time. Leaves also make carotenoids to help chlorophyll. Why are leaves green if yellow and orange pigments are present?

Look at bananas for clues. As bananas ripen, they turn from green to yellow. Yellow color is there all along. Chlorophyll hides it. When chlorophyll breaks down, yellow color shows through. What do you think will happen when photosynthesis stops in leaves?

Here leaves are starting to turn from green to their fall colors. As photosynthesis stops, the yellow and orange colors shine through.

This tree has no more chlorophyll in its leaves. The leaves have turned yellow and orange and will soon fall off the tree.

# Shutting Down

In spring and summer, plants make so much chlorophyll that it masks the other colors. In fall, it gets colder outside. There are fewer hours of daylight. These changes say winter is coming.

Plants start to close up shop. The connection between the plant and the leaves closes. In the leaf blades, photosynthesis slows, then stops. The broken-down chlorophyll is not replaced. Carotenoids do not break down as fast as chlorophyll. They hang around coloring leaves yellow and orange. During this time, plants also begin to make anthocyanins.

For the best displays of fall leaf colors, hope for sunny, warm days, cool nights, some rain, and no frost. If there is an early frost, fall colors are likely to be duller.

# Nature's Big Show

Evergreens, like pine, cedars, firs, and spruce, do not change color in fall. These plants often keep their needlelike leaves for a few years. Needles have matter inside them that acts like antifreeze to help them live through winter.

Do you live where seasons change? Then you can observe nature's big show. All **deciduous** plants have a part to play. The real stars, though, are the trees that shed their leafy costumes before winter arrives. In yellows and oranges are hickory, elm, cottonwood, black walnut, ash, larch, and others.

Not to be outdone are dogwoods, alders, and some oaks in showy shades of red. Sugar maples turn pale yellow, bright orange, and red. What players will you see on fall's stage? It depends on where you live.

Here trees show off their beautiful fall colors. The green trees in between are evergreens, which do not change color in fall.

# Leaf Detectives

Fall's brightest and deepest reds come from anthocyanins, which do not form until fall. Leaves start shutting down in fall, though. Why do they use their energy to make new pigments?

Scientists have tried to explain this mystery. They asked, "How will this matter help the plant?" Some think it keeps bugs away. Others think it acts like a sunscreen so the plant can get food from the leaves for longer.

Do you have any questions about leaves and their colors? Try to find out the answers. Start by watching the leaves as they change. Enjoy the show!

# Glossary

**anthocyanins** (an-thuh-SY-uh-nunz)  Red and blue matter inside plants.

**carbohydrates** (kar-boh-HY-drayts)  The main part in foods that are made mostly from plants.

**carbon** (KAR-bun)  An element found in all living things.

**carbon dioxide** (KAR-bin dy-OK-syd)  A gas that plants take in from the air and use to make food.

**carotenoids** (kuh-RO-teh-noydz)  Yellow and orange matter inside plants that helps photosynthesis.

**chlorophyll** (KLOR-uh-fil)  Green matter inside plants that allows them to use energy from sunlight to make their own food.

**deciduous** (deh-SIH-joo-us)  Having leaves that fall off every year.

**minerals** (MIN-rulz)  Natural things that are not animals, plants, or other living things.

**oxygen** (OK-sih-jen)  A gas that has no color, taste, or odor and is necessary for people and animals to breathe.

**photosynthesis** (foh-toh-SIN-thuh-sus)  The way in which green plants make their own food from sunlight, water, and a gas called carbon dioxide.

**pigments** (PIG-ments)  Coloring matter in animals and plants.

**reflects** (rih-FLEKTS)  Throws back light, heat, or sound.

# Index

## A
anthocyanins, 11, 19, 22

## B
blade, 12

## C
carbohydrates, 7
carbon dioxide, 4, 7
carotenoids, 11, 16, 19

## chlorophyll, 7, 8, 11, 16, 19

## M
minerals, 15

## O
oxygen, 7

## P
photosynthesis, 4, 7, 11, 12, 15–16, 19

## pigments, 11, 16, 22
pores, 12

## R
roots, 15

## S
stalk, 12
sugar(s), 7, 15

## W
water, 7, 8, 15

# Web Sites

Due to the changing nature of Internet links, PowerKids Press has developed an online list of Web sites related to the subject of this book. This site is updated regularly. Please use this link to access the list:
www.powerkidslinks.com/scidet/leaves/